Daniel Goodwin

The Dearborns

A Discourse Commemorative of the Eightieth Anniversary of the

Occupation of Fort Dearborn

Daniel Goodwin

The Dearborns
A Discourse Commemorative of the Eightieth Anniversary of the Occupation of Fort Dearborn

ISBN/EAN: 9783337267544

Printed in Europe, USA, Canada, Australia, Japan

Cover: Foto ©ninafisch / pixelio.de

More available books at **www.hansebooks.com**

Chicago Historical Society's

PROCEEDINGS.

THE DEARBORNS.

By DANIEL GOODWIN, Jr.

H. Dearborn

THE DEARBORNS;

A

DISCOURSE COMMEMORATIVE

OF THE

EIGHTIETH ANNIVERSARY OF THE OCCUPATION

OF

FORT DEARBORN,

AND THE

FIRST SETTLEMENT AT CHICAGO;

READ BEFORE THE

CHICAGO HISTORICAL SOCIETY,

TUESDAY, DEC. 18, 1883,

BY

DANIEL GOODWIN, JR.

WITH REMARKS OF

Hons. JOHN WENTWORTH, J. YOUNG SCAMMON,
E. B. WASHBURNE, and I. N. ARNOLD.

CHICAGO: ·
FERGUS PRINTING COMPANY.
1884.

CONTENTS.

CHICAGO HISTORICAL SOCIETY, 140 DEARBORN AVE.,

December 19, 1883.

Mr. DANIEL GOODWIN, Jr., 283 Erie St.,

Dear Sir:—I have the honor to enclose a copy of the reso
lution of this Society, adopted at the monthly meeting last
evening, thanking you for your discourse on the Dearborns and
asking for a copy of the same for preservation in our archives.
Also a copy of the resolution acknowledging receipt of a copy
of Gilbert Stuart's oil portrait of Major-General Henry Dearborn,
and returning the thanks of this Society to the donors—the
Messrs. Wirt Dexter, Marshall Field, John Crerar, N. K. Fair-
bank, E. W. Blatchford, Mark Skinner, and yourself.

Yours very respectfully,

ALBERT D. HAGER, Secretary.

283 ERIE STREET, CHICAGO,

March 5, 1884.

Mr. ALBERT D. HAGER, Sec. of Chicago Hist. Society,

Dear Sir:—It gives me great pleasure to comply with the
request of your Society for a copy of my discourse on "The
Dearborns" to be preserved in the archives of the Society, and
in order that the information which I have collected, concerning
those worthies of former generations, may be more widely
extended, I have caused the same to be published by the
Fergus Printing Company of this city, and have requested that
company to deliver the proceeds derived from the sale of the
same into the treasury of your Society.

Very truly yours,

DANIEL GOODWIN, Jr.

To the Chicago Historical Society:

The Undersigned herewith Present to your Society a copy of GILBERT STUART'S portrait of

MAJOR-GENERAL HENRY DEARBORN,

Captain of a New-Hampshire Regiment in the Battle of Bunker Hill;

A Soldier through the Revolutionary War from 1775 to 1783;

United States Marshal for the District of Maine under President Washington;

Secretary of War under President Jefferson;

Collector of the Port of Boston under President Madison;

General-in-Chief of the United States Army under President Monroe;

Born in New Hampshire, 1751;

Died in Boston Highlands, 1829.

Dated at Chicago, Dec. 3, 1883, upon the Eightieth Anniversary of the first occupation of Fort Dearborn at Chicago by Captain John Whistler and a Company of the First Regiment United States Infantry.

Wirt Dexter,

Marshall Field,	Daniel Goodwin, Jr.,
John Crerar,	N. K. Fairbank,
E. W. Blatchford,	Mark Skinner.

PROCEEDINGS.

THE regular monthly meeting of the Chicago Historical Society was held in its Hall, No. 142 Dearborn Avenue, on the 18th of December, 1883.

Hon. Isaac N. Arnold, president, presided, and Albert D. Hager was secretary.

The Librarian reported the receipt of a number of volumes, pamphlets, maps, and autograph letters from Messrs. Mark Skinner, William Blair, Albert A. Munger, John R. Walsh, and Daniel Goodwin, Jr.

Hon. John Wentworth reported a memorial of the life of James Sears Waterman, a member of the Society, lately deceased at Sycamore, Illinois.

The Secretary then read the foregoing memorial tablet, which was printed on parchment, with the original signatures of the donors, and handsomely framed and suspended on the wall.

The President then called upon Mr. Daniel Goodwin, Jr., the appointed orator of the evening, who delivered the following address:

THE DEARBORNS.

—

FROM the earliest days of recorded history, it has been a natural impulse of mankind to honor the names of its heroes and its loved ones, those who had taken a strong hold upon the popular heart, by giving those names to the highways of public travel. In this latest of the great aggregations of human beings are found the names of the grand founders and champions of the United States of America, marking and defining the highways thronged day and night by hosts numbered by hundreds of thousands.

As you pass from this building dedicated to history, where faithful hands are garnering up the records of the past and the present, you will find yourselves on an avenue bearing the name of one loved by Washington, trusted by Jefferson, and honored by Madison and Monroe; who not only fought with, but was the hearty friend of Lafayette and Rochambeau, of Greene and Sullivan.

I have walked along this great thoroughfare which bears his name for a quarter of a century, and have often asked myself, what were the peculiar merits of this man whose name keeps pace with my daily steps? Where did he live, what was his work, who were his friends, what was his social life, who and what were his children, how did he die, and where now rest his honored bones? These questions traveled with me unanswered until I resolved to look up the history of that first name which marked this spot when it was known only to the government as "Fort Dearborn" —a name antedating the birth and infancy of our great city; a name identified with the Indian massacre of 1812; a name which has kept pace with the growth of a frontier-post and Indian-station from a village to a city, and now, though but a half-century old, the grand metropolis of the Northwest; a name given to one of its social clubs, as well as to that scientific observatory overlooking our great harbor, and which once in our own day looked down upon 12,000 rebellious sons,[*] whose forefathers fought by the side of Henry Dearborn in the bloody fields of the Revolution or under his banner in the war of 1812—sons who, thank God, have again learned to keep step to the music of the Union!

The Dearborn family in America began with one Godfrey Dearborn, who was born in old Exeter, County of Devon, England, about the year 1600. He first came to the Massachusetts Colony about 1639, but removed to Exeter, New Hampshire—thus exchanging the Exeter of his native land for the Exeter of the wilderness. Here he remained for ten years and then moved to Hampton, where he passed the remainder of his life. On his arrival, he settled on a farm at West End, which has been occupied by his descendants until this time.

Godfrey Dearborn's eldest son, Henry, was born about 1633, in England, and came to this country with his father in 1639, and resided in Hampton until he was 92 years old. He married Elizabeth Marrian in 1666. Their oldest son, John Dearborn, settled at North Hampton, and in

---

[*] Dearborn Observatory is on a tower of the Chicago University, ninety feet high. After the capture of Fort Donelson, the rebel prisoners were brought to Chicago, and placed in camp around the University. It was called Camp. Douglas, and the number of prisoners was increased until they reached 12,000.

1689, married Abigail Bachelder. He was a deacon in the church and a strong character. He died in 1750, aged 84 years. His ninth child was Simon Dearborn, born 1706, in the garrison-house on the Green at North Hampton, where his mother had been lodged for security against the Indians who were at that time very troublesome. This Simon Dearborn married Sarah Marston in 1728, and their twelfth child, afterward known as Major-General Henry Dearborn, the chief subject of this sketch, was born at North Hampton in 1751. He grew up among the rugged hills of New Hampshire one of the finest types of manly strength, agility, and beauty. He was tall and straight, muscular and agile. He was noted as an unmatched wrestler, never having met his equal, and was an ardent sportsman. In all his journeys he carried his gun and rod and dog, and was an expert at cricket and ball until long past middle life. When not engaged in business or exercise, he was a constant reader, and was master of as good English as the war department has produced. After going through some of the best schools in New Hampshire, he began and completed a full course of medical instruction under Dr. Hall Jackson of Portsmouth, a distinguished surgeon in the army of the Revolution

Dr. Dearborn was settled in the practice of a physician at Nottingham three years prior to the Revolution. With most of the ablest young men of that vicinity, he employed all his leisure in military exercises and studying the science of war. "The spirit of the mountains was stirred." Liberty was calling out to her sons and numbering them by name, and they saw or felt that the liberties of their country would soon be either shamefully surrendered and brutally trodden under foot, or manfully defended and cruelly purchased at the sword's point and the cannon's mouth.

The great principles of political liberty had been dis-

cussed and agitated in the school-and-meeting houses of
New Hampshire, as well as in the neighboring city of
Boston, by the ablest minds and most eloquent tongues.
The whole coast of New England, from Newport Bay to
the watershed of the St. Lawrence River, was filled with a
race of men who in their words and deeds exhibited as
much genius as any set of men the world has produced.
England *alone* could not produce their equals nor their
rivals; nor could Scotland, Ireland, France, or Germany;
but the patriots of the American Revolution, with tongues
of fire, with muscles of steel, with heroism born of enthusiasm and sentiment, with clear and defined ideas of
liberty, governed by law, were the result of a century of
crossing and recrossing of the most enterprising and fear-
less men and women of all those countries combined.
The Pilgrim Fathers, who left country and home and
friends with almost broken hearts that they might worship
God in their own way, were there in the greatest propor-
tion; but the Anglo-Saxon blood, which has always developed the richest results when crossed by other races, was
mingled with the Huguenots of France, the Celts of Ireland, and the Scotch and Dutch.   Samuel Adams, the
finest type of old Puritanism, thundered in the lower and
popular assembly of the Massachusetts house, while the
genius of a French Huguenot animated and directed the
patriots of the upper house or council in James Bowdoin.
So it was in New Hampshire.   Her mountains and valleys
were peopled by races from many countries and climes;
the tame and contented had staid at home to bow the
knee to the tyranny of Stuarts and Bourbons, of Guelphs
and Hapsburgs; but the most daring and the most liberty-
loving from all the western nations of Europe had come
into this wilderness for freedom.   They married and in-
termarried, they fought the Indian and subdued the wilderness, they knew and understood and loved their political

rights; and when George the Second and his good queen
Caroline and Lord Walpole died and gave place to George
Third and his infamous cabinet, who struck down char-
tered rights a century old, stopped our commerce, deposed
our local officers, carried off our citizens for trial to a for-
eign land, imposed taxes without giving us any represen-
tation, and, in fine, treated the American colonies as her
slaves; a race of men was aroused who combined in themselves all the courage of Englishmen, the rushing energy
of the Huguenot, the dash of the Irish, the stubborn wis-
dom and endurance of the Scotch, and the firm devotion
of the Dutch. It was among such men as these that our
young Dr. Dearborn, only 24 years of age, with an iron
constitution and a stubborn will, heard the news on the
20th of April, 1775, that the British army had commenced
the war at Lexington. There was no waiting for form or
ceremony. Dearborn and sixty of his young townsfellows
only knew that their Boston brethren were in danger, and
before twenty-four hours had run their course, those sixty
young giants had marched with their own guns over their
shoulders all the way from Hampton to Cambridge, a dis-
tance of fifty-five miles. This first march as volunteer
soldiers was a fair specimen of the endurance of those
men till the seven years' war was over. After remaining
several days at Cambridge and finding that there was no
immediate need for their services, they marched home
again and continued to prepare for the desperate contest.
It was at once determined that New Hampshire should
raise several regiments for the common defence, and Dr.
Dearborn was appointed a captain in the 1st regiment,
commanded by Col. John Stark. So great was his popu-
larity that within ten days after he received his commission, he enlisted a full company and marched to Medford
on the 15th of May. He immediately began drilling his
men, carrying a gun and sword himself and doing as much

work as any of them. Upon his own responsibility, he
began skirmishing with the British for the possession of
the cattle and stock on Noddles Island, and he and his
company had two fights with the enemy before the battle
of Bunker Hill. On the 16th of June, it was determined
that a fortified post should be established at or near
Bunker Hill. The decision and its execution led on the
following day to the battle. Col. Stark's regiment was
quartered in Medford about four miles from the point of
anticipated attack. About ten o'clock in the morning, he
received orders to march. The regiment formed in front
of the arsenal, and each man, Captain Dearborn among
them, received a gill-cup full of powder, fifteen balls, and
one flint. After making all necessary preparations for
action, they marched about one o'clock, and about two,
they were stationed about forty yards in the rear of the
redoubt toward Mystic River. They were soon engaged
in a heavy action, and Capt. Dearborn stood with his men,
all of whom were practised shots, and he and they did
terrible execution with steady nerves and quick eyes.
Such a battle was never seen before and is not likely to be
seen again. The number of Americans in action did not
exceed 1500; and they killed or wounded nearly as many
as their whole number, with a loss of but 145 killed and
304 wounded. Again and again did the brave Britons
march up against that wall of fire, only to fall back with
many of their officers and most of their men bleeding or
dead, until at length the ammunition of the 1500 Americans was exhausted, and no reënforcements of men or
powder or bayonets were sent them, though Putnam and
Gerrish were within easy reach and could have gone to
them by the same road over which the tired fighters were
obliged to retreat, and the British flag floated over the
hill which, as many orators have said, cost Britain a continent.

Soon after this terrible battle, it was decided to send an expedition to Quebec with a view of taking that Gibraltar of North America, and thus commanding the St. Lawrence and aiding the Canadas to join the patriot revolution. Colonel Benedict Arnold was selected to lead this desperate expedition, and Dearborn volunteered to command a company. He was allowed to select a picked company from the New-Hampshire regiment for this arduous service. Capt. Dearborn kept a daily journal of the expedition, and the original manuscript is now in the Boston Public Library. Through the courtesy of Judge Chamberlain, I was recently permitted to occupy a table in their directors' room, made superb by the marble busts and portraits of many of the greatest of Massachusetts' dead, and I copied the record of that march from the brown old pages which the young soldier penned more than 100 years ago. It was a march attended by every hardship which human nature is capable of enduring — bodily fatigue, desertion of three whole companies of men, loss of ammunition and guns and baggage, fording streams as cold as ice, braving tempests; and at last, famished and starving, less than half of the brave fellows who started reached the St. Lawrence River. Dearborn was prostrated by a fever for thirty days in a rude hut with no medicine or attendance save that of a French boy. On the 9th December, he rejoined his company, who had supposed him dead. Then came the attack on Quebec; the death of Montgomery; the wounding of Arnold; the failure of the attack; their capture; his confinement at Quebec, where they all had the small-pox and most of them were put in irons. In May, 1776, he was released on parole, and, after hardships nearly as great as those attending the expedition, he reached his home in July.

The next chapter of Dearborn's career began in January, 1777. On the 24th, he was exchanged and relieved

from his parole, and on the very next day, he left his wife
and children and repaired to the main army at New York,
where he was made major of the 3d New-Hampshire Regiment under Col. Scammell, that brave bachelor whom
Daniel Webster said he could never read of without being much affected. On the 10th of May, he set out for
Ticonderoga and arrived on the 20th, and took part in
that council of war where the brave but unfortunate
St. Clair was obliged to retire before an overwhelming
fleet and army. Dearborn, no braver but more fortunate
than his general, retreated from Ticonderoga through the
Green Mountains of Vermont, a circuit of more than 150
miles to Saratoga, and took conspicuous part in the
famous capture of the same army and general who had
driven them out of Ticonderoga. Most of us have read
of that series of remarkable battles in the glowing pages
of your distinguished president, Mr. Arnold.

Dearborn's old yellow diary says, "Aug. 11. I am
appointed to the command of 300 light infantry who are
drafted from the several regiments in the Northern army
to act in conjunction with Col. Morgan's corps of Rifle-
men." A strong position was selected, called Bemis
Heights, and occupied by the American army. The rifle-
men and Dearborn's corps of light infantry encamped in
advance to the left of the main line. The British army
had advanced from Saratoga and encamped on the bank
of the river within three miles of Gates' position. On the
19th of September, the right wing of the British army
moved, when Morgan and Dearborn, who commanded
separate corps, received orders from Arnold to make a
forward movement and check them. These orders were
promptly obeyed and the charge was led by Dearborn in
person in the most gallant and determined manner. The
action at once became general and continued till night on
the same ground on which it began; neither party having

retreated more than thirty rods, so that the dead of both armies were mingled together.

On the 7th of October, Burgoyne determined to make a last effort to gain possession of the American position and to open a passage for his army to Albany, where he expected to join the British forces which had gained command of the Hudson River. About ten o'clock, he advanced with a fine train of artillery, and after driving in our pickets appeared in full view on the left of Gates' line in open ground. Morgan and Dearborn were ordered by Arnold to advance and hold the enemy in check. They advanced rapidly, and in a few minutes, were engaged with the enemy; but soon after received orders to move in such a direction as to meet and oppose any body of the enemy that might try to occupy the eminence commanding our left wing. In this movement about 500 of the enemy under Earl Balcarres were met and dispersed by one fire and bayonet charge led by Dearborn himself. Balcarres reformed behind a fence, and being again attacked by Dearborn, Morgan, and Gen. Poor's brigade, the whole British line, commanded by Burgoyne in person, gave way and retired to their camp. Dearborn bore directly on the rear of the right wing, where the British artillery was posted under cover of some German troops, ran rapidly up to the pieces, and when within thirty yards, threw in such a deadly fire as to kill and disperse the whole covering party, as well as most of the artillery-men. The artillery was captured. Maj. Williams, its commander, was killed, and Sir Francis Clarke and other officers were wounded. Dearborn sent Clarke, one of Burgoyne's aids, to his own tent, where he died that night, first giving his pistols to Dearborn, a pair of most memorable arms, which now hang over the library door of his grandson, Henry G. R. Dearborn, in Roxbury. Instantly upon taking the cannon, Dearborn sent them round to the right of the

British army, then advanced his line within sixty yards of the enemy's rear, and poured in a full fire from his whole corps, which drove the enemy in great disorder to their fortified camp. The whole American army then advanced upon the British; and while Arnold, with Dearborn's corps and several regiments of infantry, assaulted and carried the German fortified camp on the right, Gen. Poor and his New-Hampshire line attacked Fraser's camp, which the enemy abandoned. It was then nearly dark. In the assault on the German camp, Arnold, who leaped his horse over the ramparts, received a severe wound in his leg and his horse fell upon him, dead. Dearborn ran to him and helped him from under his horse and asked him if he was badly hurt. He answered with great warmth, "Yes, in the same leg that was wounded at Quebec. I can never go into action without being shot. I wish the ball had gone through my heart."

Early next morning, Dearborn's corps, with about 1000 infantry, advanced over the field of battle into the rear of the enemy's main position to prevent Burgoyne from retreating toward Canada. Next day began the great retreat of the whole British force, which was so vigorously followed up by our light troops and victorious patriots that on the 19th, the whole British army was captured and surrendered. The entry in Dearborn's journal, October 19, is, "This day the great Mr. Burgoyne with his whole army surrendered themselves as prisoners of war with all their public stores; and after grounding their arms, marched off for New England. The greatest conquest ever known. The campaign has cost the British 10,250 men, forty-seven pieces of brass artillery, and a vast quantity of stores, baggage, etc."

It is a remarkable circumstance that one of the British prisoners taken with Burgoyne was the John Whistler, who afterward joined the American army and was stationed at Detroit in 1803 under Major Pike, came here that summer and built Fort Dearborn, commanded and lived in it for many years, and had two children born here.

Gen. Gates, in his official report of the battle of Saratoga, especially praised the bravery and good conduct of Dearborn. He was promoted to be lieutenant-colonel, his special corps of light infantry was broken up, and the several officers went back to their own regiments.

In the meantime, we had lost forts Montgomery and Clinton on the Hudson, and the British were coming up the river and burning its towns; and before resting from their terrible efforts with Burgoyne, the whole New-Hampshire line was ordered to make all speed to Albany, to check the progress of the British up the river. They marched that forty miles over muddy roads, and forded the Mohawk River below the falls in fourteen hours, carrying both artillery and baggage-wagons. It was the most remarkable march of the war and it saved Albany; for Clinton at once turned and went back to the City of New York.

Before the year was over, we find our young hero in a new field of war under the eye of that greatest of leaders, Gen. Washington himself, at Germantown. In the first week of December, 1777, he was constantly skirmishing and fighting with the unconquerable brigade of New Hampshire, which, as Daniel Webster said at the great banquet of New-Hampshire Sons in Boston in 1849, "left their honored dead on every battle-field of the Revolution."

Dearborn's journal says, "Dec. 7. The enemy retreated toward Germantown and into Philadelphia, which must convince the world that Mr. Howe did not dare to fight us unless he could have the advantage of the ground. Dec. 18. Thanksgiving Day through the whole continent of America, but God knows we have very little to keep

2

it with, this being the 3d day we have been without flour
or bread, and are living on a high uncultivated hill in huts
and tents, laying on the cold ground. Upon the whole, I
think all we have to be thankful for, is that we are alive and
not in the grave with so many of our friends. We had
for Thanksgiving breakfast some exceeding poor beef,
which had been boiled, and now warmed in an old frying-
pan, in which we were obliged to eat it, having no plates.
I dined or supped at Gen. Sullivan's today, and so ended
Thanksgiving. Dec. 19. The army marched about five
miles and encamped near a height, where we are to build
huts to live in this winter. Dec. 31. Having obtained
leave from Gen. Washington, I intend to set out for home
next Sunday. God grant me a happy sight of my friends."

"1778, Jan. 3. Received my commission as lieut.-col. to
Col. Scammell and sent out for home. 18th. Arrived safe
home and found all well." Here follow several lines erased
and scrawled over, as if some bit of tenderness had fallen
from that young soldier's heart at meeting again his wife
and two little girls, too sacred for any stranger eye.

On the 22d of April, he again left his little brood and
joined the main army at Valley Forge. On the 17th of
May, he says, "I dined at Gen. Washington's. May 19.
A detachment of 2000 men marched out today, commanded by Marquis Lafayette." Here follow several
pages of vivid description of the battle of Monmouth.
Dearborn's regiment first acted under orders from Lee,
until the army was thrown into confusion and began to
retreat, when Washington in person turned the tide and
converted the defeat into a victory. On this change of
battle, Dearborn received his orders directly from the
mouth of Washington. He ends by saying, "The enemy's
loss in the battle was 327 killed, 500 wounded, and 95
prisoners. Our loss, 63 killed, 210 wounded. Here ends
the famous battle of Monmouth."

In the general orders of the next day, Washington
bestowed the highest commendation on the brilliant
exploit of the New-Hampshire regiment. Col. Brooks,
the adjutant of Lee's division, afterward governor of Massachusetts, declared that the gallant conduct of the New
Hampshire regiment was the salvation of the army and
turned the tide from defeat to victory.

In 1779, Col. Dearborn was at one time in command of
the forces at New London and was moving from place to
place through Connecticut, New Jersey, and Pennsylvania,
being in April in command of a whole brigade, and then
accompanied Gen. Sullivan's expedition against the Six
Nations of Indians in Western New York. In 1780, he
was with the main army in New Jersey, and attended the
funeral of his old commander and brother-in-law, Gen.
Poor, described as the most magnificent and solemn
through the war. In 1781, he was made a quartermaster-
general, and served with Washington in Virginia, and was
at the siege of Yorktown and the capture of Cornwallis
and his army, where he lost his dearly-loved friend, Col.
Scammell, the popular adjutant of the army and for whom
both he and Gov. Brooks named their sons. In 1782, he
was at Newburgh, N.Y., and from thence in camp at Saratoga, where, on November 3d, he says, "We hear from
headquarters that a general peace is very nearly agreed
upon." He was ordered to New York and embarked his
regiment on the 16th for Newburgh, where they encamped
for the winter. In June, 1783, the New-Hampshire line
was reduced to one regiment; and on the 10th, he was
honorably discharged after eight years of the most active
service.

From his twenty-fourth to his thirty-third year, Henry
Dearborn was personally present and personally fought
with gun and sword at Bunker Hill, Quebec, Saratoga,
Monmouth, and Yorktown. His commanders were as

varied as the territory over which he fought. Stark,
Arnold, St. Clair, Gates, Greene, Sullivan, and Washington,
all saw his gallant conduct, and he had the confidence and
approbation of them all. Of the thirteen captains, who
began with Dearborn in the gallant New-Hampshire brigade, only Col. Reid remained with him till the close of
the war. Twenty-five years after the war, Gen. Reid was
sheriff and attending court at Exeter. He said, "I saw
a carriage passing and heard a voice exclaim, 'Hello,
George!' I looked up and answered, 'Harry, is that you?'
We went to the hotel together and had a grand time. I
had not seen him for twenty-five years." A gentleman
present, said, "Gen. Reid, how could you get along with
such a democrat as Gen. Dearborn is?" Reid paused a
moment and said, "I always was sorry Harry was a democrat, but that is of no consequence among old officers.
He is a noble fellow; there is no man I esteem and love
more, and if Jefferson had always made as good appoint-
ments as Dearborn to the war-office, I should think much
better of him than I do now."

Many old accounts and receipts, and some stirring war-
songs and tender bits of love and sentiment fill the pages
in the back of Dearborn's diary; songs and ballads which
cheered the lonely hut or breezy tent, while cold and
hunger, the loss of brave comrades, and the awful uncer-
tainties of the future, were weighing down those brave
spirits who fought *our* battles, and gained for *us* a free
land, one hundred years ago.

In March, 1783, Col. Dearborn wrote in his journal,
"Here ends my military life." In that same month was
born to him in his home in Exeter his first and the only
son who survived him. I have purposely omitted the sad
record in 1778, which told of the illness of his young wife,
of the eleven long days of travel from the camp to his
home, of her death and funeral, of his parting with his

two little girls, and his return to the battle-field. His first
wife was Mary, daughter of Gen. Bartlett of New Hampshire. In 1780, he married Dorcas, daughter of Col. Osgood
of Andover, and this marriage was blessed, during his last
year of Revolutionary service, by the birth of that son
whose love made the sunshine of his old age, and whose
genius adorned the halls and rostrums, and beautified the
hills and valleys of New England. One of the supremest
blessings, vouchsafed by the Great Father who made us,
that of seeing his own son grow up by his side, gifted,
good, and loving, denied to Washington, to Jefferson, to
Samuel Adams, was not denied to Dearborn. In 1784,
he moved his family to Pittson, on the Kennebec River.*

* When General Dearborn went up the Kennebec River on the expedition to
Quebec, in 1775, he was so impressed by the beauty of the country that soon
after the war, in 1784, he decided to settle at Pittston, the head of its naviga-
tion. The town of Pittston, which then included all of Gardiner and Pittston, was named for James Pitts of Boston. The whole valley of the Kennebec, from its mouth to Augusta, belonged to the Kennebec Company. John
Adams in his diary, February 15, 1771, says: "I am going tonight to Mr.
Pitts' to meet the Kennebec Co.—Bowdoin, Gardiner, Hallowell, and Pitts.
There I shall hear philosophy and politics in perfection from H.; high flying,
high church, high state from G.; sedate, cool moderation from B.; and warm,
honest, frank whigism from P." Mr. Pitts' house then stood where the
Howard Athenæum now stands. The town of Pittston was laid out in eleven
farms, fronting one mile wide each on the river, and five miles deep, which
were set off to Benjamin Hallowell, Samuel Goodwin, Francis Whitmore,
Rev. Mr. Stone, Wm. Bowdoin, Thomas Hancock, James Pitts, and James
Bowdoin. It was first called Gardiner, after one of the Kennebec Co., but
he sided with the Tories and left the country, and the citizens demanded a
change of name to some patriot. The bill to incorporate the town passed
the Massachusetts House in January, 1779. John Pitts, the oldest son of
James, was then speaker of the House. Another son, Lendall Pitts, was
leader of the tea party (Drake's "Old Land-marks of Boston," p. 498), and
in honor of their family, the town was named Pittston. The only daughter
of James Pitts married Col. Jonathan Warner of Portsmouth (Wentworth's
Gen., vol. 1, p. 316), who was with Stark and Dearborn in the Revolutionary War.

The only child of John Pitts married Robert Brinley, whose father lived
many years in the celebrated "Brinley Place," which Gen. Dearborn bought

Immediately on the organization of the government, President Washington appointed him U. S. marshal for the District of Maine in 1790. The State of Massachusetts appointed him a major-general of militia, he having first been elected by the field-officers. He was elected member of Congress in 1792 and 1795, and notwithstanding his devotion to Gen. Washington, he opposed the Jay treaty as being derogatory to the honor of his country—a treaty which gave us nothing and assured us nothing.

In 1794, Louis Philippe, afterward king of France, and Talleyrand visited General Dearborn at Pittston, and remained several days. Talleyrand fell into the river

in 1809 and where he or his son lived until about 1850. Mr. Thomas C. Amory, the grandson and historian of General Sullivan, told me that he went there when a boy, in 1825, as a friend of young H. G. R. Dearborn, to see the Marquis Lafayette and a grand company of notables at dinner. This house was the headquarters of General Ward, commander-in-chief, in 1775.

When Gen. H. A. S. Dearborn completed the erection of Fort Preble, in Portland Harbor, it was placed under the command of Thomas Pitts of the U. S. 4th Artillery, a grandson of James Pitts, and his 1st-lieutenant, Augustus Hobart, was a grandson of Gen. Henry Dearborn—son of Sophie Dearborn and Dudley Hobart. This company served under Dearborn on the St. Lawrence River in 1812–3, and young Hobart was killed by a cannonball. While at Fort Preble, in 1810, Maj. Thomas Pitts had a son born in the fort, the late Samuel Pitts of Detroit. After Samuel Pitts had graduated at Harvard and studied law with Judge Story, he went to Detroit about 1833 with a letter of introduction from Gen. H. A. S. Dearborn to Gen. Charles Larned, who had served under the elder Dearborn in the war of 1812. Larned was major of a Kentucky regiment under Gen. Harrison, which was incorporated into the regular army and stationed at Detroit. He was mustered out in 1816 and remained in Detroit the remainder of his life, and reared a large and influential family there. One of his sons-in-law was Gen. Alpheus S. Williams, who distinguished himself in the Mexican war and in the war of the rebellion. He was father-in-law of the late-lamented and talented Col. Francis U. Farquhar of the regular army. Mr. Pitts succeeded to General Larned's business and was his executor and trustee. Another of General Larned's pupils and a partner for some time of Mr. Pitts was Senator Jacob M. Howard, a lawyer of most eminent ability, whose eloquence was admired by almost every citizen of Michigan.

while fishing at Hallowell, and was saved by a little boy holding to him his fishing-rod.

Gen. Dearborn, while in Congress, established such a reputation as a speaker and political leader that, when the federal party under John Adams was supplanted by the republican party in 1801, President Jefferson at once invited Gen. Dearborn into his cabinet as secretary of war. It was the highest compliment which could well be paid to any man, for at that time the cabinet consisted of only four—the secretary of state, of war, of the treasury, and of the navy; and it was especially marked because the office had been filled under Adams by Samuel Dexter, one of the greatest men our country has produced. His fame as a lawyer has been placed upon the highest pinnacle by Webster, Story, and Sargent, and his administrative power was such that John Adams said of him in a letter to Vanderkemp, May 26, 1816, "I have lost the ablest friend I had on earth in Mr. Dexter." Although Mr. Dexter was one of the leaders of the federal party, President Jefferson retained him in his cabinet as secretary of the treasury for nearly a year. It was a marked tribute to the ability of a great opponent, whose presence and advice at Washington must have been peculiarly gratifying to Gen. Dearborn, who was thus easily inducted into the office of secretary of war, which he filled from 1801 to 1809.*

It was during this period that the point of land now occupied by Chicago was selected for a fort and was first used by white men as a home. Hon. John Wentworth's exhaustive paper on Fort Dearborn, published in 1881, has Dearborn's letter to Gen. Wilkinson in 1804, stating his views on the best mode of protecting our frontier.

* It is peculiarly fitting and appropriate that the list of donors of the oil portrait of Gen. Henry Dearborn, given to this Society, should be headed by Mr. Dexter, a grandson of the secretary of war under Adams, who preceded Dearborn as secretary of war under Jefferson.

Gen. James Grant Wilson published an article in 1862,
saying that Fort Dearborn was first occupied by Capt.
John Whistler and a company of the First Regiment of
U. S. Infantry on December 3d, 1803.   He has recently
furnished me a letter not published, written in April, 1803,
by the Abbotts of Detroit to Abbott and Maxwell of
Mackinac, saying that Capt. Whistler had gone to Chicago
with troops to erect a fort.*   In the Army Report of Dec.
31, 1803, Fort Dearborn is included as one of the national
forts.   Gen. Wilson says he had it from Dr. John Cooper,
stationed at Fort Dearborn in 1808, and that he had it
from Capt. Whistler that the fort was first occupied on the
3d of December, 1803.   At that time there was but one
other house in Chicago, a log-cabin on the north-side,
owned and occupied by Pierre LeMay, a French-Canadian
trader, and his Indian wife.

The log-cabin and the fort of 1803 have given place to
this collosal emporium, and when, twenty years hence, our
successors shall celebrate the one-hundredth anniversary
of the first occupation of Fort Dearborn, it will undoubt-
edly be among a million of people in a city far surpassing

---

* NEW YORK, 23 Nov., 1883.

MY DEAR GOODWIN:—My authority for the statement that Fort Dearborn was occupied on the third of December, 1803, is the war department,
confirmed by Dr. John Cooper, who was stationed at Fort Dearborn as surgeon's-mate as early as 1808.

Among other unpublished manuscripts in my possession, which I hope soon
to use in a reliable History of Chicago, is a letter dated "Detroit, April 30,
1803," which says: "The Cincinnati mail arrived here two days ago, and
brings accounts of a garrison being immediately erected at Chicago.   Capt.
Whistler is to have command of the garrison, and will leave this in a few
days with his company, which consists of 80 men, to go and erect the garrison.   This is a good opening for you if you wish to extend your trade.   Captain Whistler wishes that we could send a store there.

P. S. since writing.—Capt. Whistler has only taken six men with him to
go and examine the ground and report to Major Pike, here."

The writers of the letter were Robert and James Abbott, a firm of Detroit

in commerce, wealth, and grandeur any city of the world
prior to the present century.

Gen. Dearborn's administration of the war department
was acceptable to the whole country. When he left the
office, a committee of political opponents examined his
department and reported everything correct. President
Madison appointed him collector of the port of Boston in
1809. During this year, his grandson, Henry G. R., was
born in the old Brinley Place at Roxbury, near which he
now lives and where he treasures the admirable portraits
of his father and grandfather by Gilbert Stuart; the arms,
badges, and commissions made historic by brave deeds;
and many shelves of manuscript letters, books, and docu-
mentary records of the wars of 1776 and 1812.

While Gen. Dearborn was secretary of war, his son, the
younger general, had spent two years at Williams College,
Mass., and two years at William & Mary's College, Va.,
and had studied law with Judge Story at Salem. Here,
in 1807, when twenty-four years of age, he married the
daughter of Col. William Raymond Lee. He had already

merchants, and it is addressed to Abbott & Maxwell, merchants at Michili-
mackinac.   *   *   *   Very faithfully yours,

JAS. GRANT WILSON.

Dr. Cooper's statement to Gen. Wilson is corroborated by the claim of
Major Wm. Whistler (see Wentworth's "Early Chicago," p. 12) that he
came here in 1803, as a second lieutenant in his father's company. Also by
the statement of Mrs. Wm. Whistler, quoted by Mr. Wentworth, p. 13, ib.,
from H. H. Hurlbut's "Chicago Antiquities," that she was married to Lieut.
Wm. Whistler in 1802, and that in the summer of 1803, Capt. Whistler's
company was ordered from Detroit to Chicago to occupy the post and build
the fort; that she and her young husband and his father and Mrs. Whistler
came to Chicago by the U. S. schooner *Tracy*, and the company came over-
land conducted by Lieut. James S. Swearingen. That the fort was finished and
occupied in 1803, is certain from the fact that the army return of December 31,
1803, states the number of officers and men on duty at Fort Dearborn Chicago, Illinois Territory. See also "American State Papers," Vol. I., p. 175.

commenced public life by superintending the construction
and armament of the forts in Portland Harbor.

In 1812, a second war of independence was forced upon
us by an accumulation of insult and injury, which drove
the people to arms, notwithstanding the protest and opposition of New England. The Jay treaty had failed to
bring us anything like fair treatment from Great Britain.
They boarded our vessels and impressed thousands upon
thousands of our best seamen; they refused to give up
the forts within our territories on the Northwest frontier;
and made them rallying points for swarms of Indian savages, who plundered, burned, killed, tortured, and scalped
men, women, and children with indiscriminate brutality.

In January, 1812, Congress passed an act adding 20,000
to our military establishment and providing for two major-
generals and five brigadier-generals, and at once President
Madison asked Dearborn to accept the first appointment
as senior major-general; and the man who wrote in 1783,
"Here ends my military life," was called, twenty-nine years
later, to again buckle on his sword. "Our eyes," wrote
Madison, "could not but be turned to your qualifications
and experience. I hope you will so far suspend all other
considerations as not to withhold your consent, as quickly
as possible." Gen. Dearborn informed the president that
his life had been devoted to the service of his country,
and he felt himself bound to obey her commands when-
ever his services were required. He was then appointed,
and on the 28th of January, was confirmed, and the very
day after receipt of the appointment, he left Roxbury for
Washington. His son, Henry Alexander Scammell Dearborn, though but twenty-nine years old, was appointed
collector of the port of Boston, commandant of the forts,
and general of the local military forces there. Gen. Dearborn, at Washington, at once laid out the plans of an
active campaign on the northern and northwestern frontier,

and in person at Albany directed the establishment of barracks, depots of arms and provisions, and the whole material of war. From there he went to Boston and adopted all the measures possible for putting the garrisons and sea-coasts of Connecticut, Rhode Island, Massachusetts, New Hampshire, and Maine in the best posture of defence.

A declaration of war was made by Congress on the 18th of June, 1812; but it was regarded by many as only a threat to bring Great Britain to face the necessity of treating us fairly or be involved in war. There was almost universal opposition to the war in Massachusetts and most of New England; and when General Dearborn called upon Governor Caleb Strong for troops to aid the federal government, the governor, under the unanimous advice of the Supreme Court of Massachusetts, refused the call as being unwarranted by the Constitution. They took the ground that the State authorities alone were the judges of when the necessity had arisen to arm in defence of the general welfare, and they were heartily opposed to being forced into a war with Great Britain, to the utter destruction, as they thought, of their commercial interests. This opinion prevailed in many of the states, and with most disastrous effects, for at some of the most critical points of the war, certain state troops refused to cross the line between their own State and Canada. The moment Gov. Strong saw danger of invasion of his own State, in defiance of the wishes of his party and his Supreme Court, he entered into hearty coöperation with both Gen. Dearborn and his son, and so thoroughly manned the forts and harbors that the British fleet, which disgracefully burned Portland and other peaceful cities on the coast, did not venture to attack old Boston. It was neither the first nor the last time that old Elder Strong's blood and brains furnished the right man in the right place for his country's honor, as the roll-call of the Army of the Tennessee in

our own day will testify.* It is one of the misfortunes
necessarily incident to our free republican government
that when war is forced upon us, it finds us unprepared
in training and discipline to cope with the veteran officers
and soldiers of arbitrary governments, who maintain stand-
ing armies; and another is that the secretary of war and
Congress and the public through the newspapers, each in
turn try to take the direction of the war. In the war of
1812, we commenced with a few old Revolutionary soldiers, few of whom had seen service for twenty five years,
and then only as colonels. Although Dearborn and his
associates had laid out a careful plan by which Hull was
to command independently on the Northwestern frontier,
and Van Rensellaer on the Niagara frontier, and Dearborn
on the Northeastern frontier, with headquarters at Albany
or Sackett's Harbor, intending to move down the St. Lawrence and take Montreal and Quebec, repeating the vision-
ary experiment of 1776, no sooner had the fight begun
than the secretary of war began to direct the whole
machinery at Washington. We had no telegraph system
by which organized and coöperative action could at once
be secured, and no railroads or steamboats, and relied only
upon the man and his horse for conveying orders over a
frontier of over two thousand miles. The surrender of our
fort and army at Detroit,† the destruction of Fort Dear-

---

* Benjamin W. Dwight, LL.D., in his History of the Strong family, has a
list of nearly a thousand of the descendants of Elder John Strong of North-
ampton, who have been soldiers and officers in the army and navy. Among
others are Gen. Thos. E. G. Ransom, Gen. Thomas J. Strong, Gen. James
Clark Strong, Col. James F. Dwight, and Richard Stanley Tuthill, U. S.
Attorney at Chicago. The special reference in the text is to a member of
this Society, Gen. William Emerson Strong, who is in the seventh generation
from Elder Strong. From captain of a Wisconsin company he rose to be
inspector-general of the Army of the Tennessee. Since 1867, he has resided
in Chicago, and been a contributor to this Society.

† A most admirable review of Gen. Hull's surrender, trial, and conviction
forms the eleventh chapter of Chief-Justice James V. Campbell's "Political
History of Michigan."

born and the massacre of its garrison and the men, women,
and children who then dwelt on the spot where we now
live, are subjects too familiar to us all and too painful to
dwell upon. The effect of these disasters was to upset
all of Dearborn's plans. But the terrible disasters of our
western departments, though it changed his plans, did not
check the energy of Gen. Dearborn, and during the winter
of 1812 and 1813, he was employed in recruiting and drilling for the coming year, and he raised around him and
drilled into useful service some of the most magnificent
young officers our country has produced: Scott, Taylor,
Wool, Brady, Ripley, Gaines, and others. His expeditious
movements in 1813, with the regular army, preserved Sackett's Harbor when abandoned by the militia, and secured
our fleet from destruction by the British. In April, though
so prostrated with sickness and fever that he had to be
carried from his bed to his horse, he commanded in person at the battle of York, resulting in the first great victory of the war, when we captured the enemy's stores and
several gun-boats.

Then came the attack upon Niagara and Fort George,
and the taking of those strongholds. In the meantime,
Gen. Lewis, the brother-in-law of Armstrong, the new
secretary of war, was plotting to secure the removal of
Gen. Dearborn, and during a severe fit of fever, he was
relieved by order of the secretary "until his health should
be reinstated." By the time the order was received, July
14, 1813, the iron constitution of the general had conquered the disease, and he was rapidly convalescing. The
indignation of his brilliant staff of officers was great; they
immediately met and addressed a letter to him, which,
considering the men who wrote it, was quite remarkable.
They declared "that in their judgment the circumstances
render his continuance with the army of the first import-
ance, if not indispensable to the good of the service. The
knowledge we possess of your numerous services in the

ardent struggles of our glorious Revolution, not to speak
of more recent events, has given us infinitely higher confidence in your ability to command with energy and effect
than we can possibly feel in ourselves or in those who will
be placed in stations of increased responsibility by your
withdrawal from this army. We earnestly entreat you to
continue in the command which you have already held
with honor to yourself and country." But Gen. Dearborn
did not feel at liberty to continue in command. The secretary of war went to the field of operations and under-
took the command himself with great discredit to our arms.

Gen. Dearborn at once retired and demanded a court of
inquiry, but so soon as President Madison learned of his
restoration to health, he appointed him to the command
of the district of New York, which was the heart of the
continent, and was threatened by the British with the fate
of Eastport and Washington, and when Congress proposed
to increase the army by 30,000, he determined to appoint
Dearborn general-in-chief of the whole army. But a general peace was declared in January—a peace which settled
the independence of America on a sure footing. Though
Great Britain did not confess her errors, she abandoned
the claims for which we went to war, and she learned a
respect for us as a nation, which she had never shown
before. The victory of Perry on Lake Erie, when, for the
first and only time in her history, an entire British fleet
was captured or destroyed in a fair fight, the conquests of
Harrison and Scott, the capture of York and forts George
and Niagara, our magnificent victories at sea by the *Constitution* over the *Guerriere*, by the *Wasp* over the *Frolic*,
by the *United States* over the *Macedonia*, by the *Constitution* over the *Java*, and the final crushing defeat at New
Orleans, had taught Great Britain to respect the rabble
whom she looked upon before as rebels fit for the toma-
hawk of the savage. The best writers and the noblest
orators in Great Britain condemned the barbarous destruc-

tion of our capital, which found no parallel even in the bloody Bonaparte, who had taken and held, and left uninjured nearly every capital in Europe; and they condemned with indignation the practice of employing against us the savages who burned our homes and slaughtered our women and children. "Willingly," said the *London Statesman*, "would we throw a vail of oblivion over our transactions at Washington. The Cossacks spared Paris, but we spared not the capital of America." The British Annual Register denounced the proceedings "as a return to the times of barbarism!"

The last war with Great Britain closed with just such a thunder-crash as that with which the first war began. The gallant Packingham, with an army of veterans fresh from the victories of Europe, with valor equal to that which breasted the fires of Bunker Hill, staggered vainly against the breastworks of our undisciplined but brave army at New Orleans, until more than two thousand were killed or wounded, while Jackson's loss was but eight killed and thirteen wounded.

Bunker Hill and New Orleans! The *Alpha* and *Omega* of war with Great Britain taught the British government that there was a race beyond the sea with too much of her own blood and brains and love of liberty to be ever conquered upon its own soil.

Gen. Dearborn immediately retired to the comforts of private life. In 1813, thirty-seven years of public service found him as poor as when he began, when he married Sarah Bowdoin, daughter of William Bowdoin and widow of James Bowdoin, the munificent patron of Bowdoin College, which has furnished our city with many of its most gifted orators.* The elder general gave up to the younger the old Brinley Place at Roxbury, and lived in the Bow-

* Judge Thomas Drummond, Hon. John N. Jewett, Hon. Melville W. Fuller, George Payson, and John J. Herrick.

doin mansion on Milk Street in Boston until 1826, with
the exception of two years spent abroad.* President Monroe appointed him minister to Portugal in 1822, and he
was unanimously confirmed. His home from 1815 to
1826 was one of the centres of all that was interesting in
art and letters and society. His wife's great wealth and
unbounded charity, his own friendship with all the famous
men of America, formed either in the army or during his
twelve years at Washington brought him to the front at
all the banquets and dinners and public meetings of Boston. Here he was visited by Lafayette, who, as a token
of esteem, gave to his daughter, the beautiful Mrs. Wingate, a set of china which had belonged to Marie Antoin-
ette. Threescore years and ten, with all their storms and
exposure, failed to bow his head, and with the same stately
dignity which many of us remember in his favorite adjutant, Winfield Scott, he bore up until his seventy-ninth
year, and then died in the home and in the arms of his
only son.

* Bowdoin Block, corner of Milk and Hawley Streets, now occupies the
site of the old mansion where so many notabilities were entertained and where
was born, in 1809, Hon. Robert C. Winthrop, selected by Congress as the
leading representative orator of the United States to deliver the oration at
Yorktown, October 19, 1881. The Dearborns gave a grand ball in this house,
July 3, 1817, for President Monroe. The visit of Monroe to Boston was a
brilliant ovation, the whole city, without distinction of party, joining in
parades, balls, illuminations, and receptions. Gen. Dearborn was chairman
of the committee. Commodores Bainbridge, Hull, and Perry were there with
war vessels; also Generals Brooks, Sullivan, Sumner, Crane, Wells, Blake,
Thorndike, Perkins, and a throng of other officers and military companies.
A great meeting was had at Bunker Hill on the 4th of July, where Monroe
expressed a sentiment similar to that of Lincoln at Gettysburg: "The blood
spilt here roused the whole American people and united them in a common
cause in defence of their rights—that union will never be broken." He
visited Cambridge, and was welcomed by President Kirkland and all the
faculty and students of Harvard. Then followed a great military parade on
the common. Harrison Gray Otis gave a party and fire-works display.
Dearborn, Otis, Quincy, and Gray dined with Monroe at Ex-President John
Adams.

PART II.

TIME compels me to hurry through the career of the younger Dearborn more rapidly than I wish, for it was a life not only of remarkable energy, but full of interest and beauty. Placed by the affection of President Madison in the most lucrative and influential federal office in New England before he was thirty years of age, he so ably conducted himself in it as to be retained there through all the administrations of Madison, Monroe, and John Quincy Adams.

Upon his removal by Jackson in 1829, he was elected to the Massachusetts legislature and placed in the executive council. Next year he was elected senator from Norfolk and member of the State constitutional convention; in 1832, member of Congress. He was appointed adjt.-general of the State of Massachusetts in 1835, and held that office until 1843. In 1847, he was elected mayor of Roxbury, and was annually reëlected until his death in 1851. In these public, official, and political positions, he conducted himself with so much energy, fairness, and ability that no partisan ever charged him with any want of patriotism, diligence, or fidelity.* In this, perhaps, he was not singular. Massachusetts has had other such public servants and officers, but while Gen. Dearborn faithfully attended his official duties, he performed an amount of

---

* Arthur W. Austin, Esq., at a meeting at West Roxbury, August 5, 1851, said: "It has been my fortune through almost the whole of my life to be ranked among the political antagonists of General Dearborn, but I have never heard his integrity in any quarter questioned or impeached, or anything advanced in derogation of his claim to entire personal respect.

"In his characteristics there was nothing selfish, interested, or mercenary; having a value in himself that which was outward did not seem to affect him."

3

public service for the world at large, without fee or reward, which can hardly be matched. Bunker-Hill Monument, the Hoosac Tunnel, the Horticultural Society, Mount Auburn, and Forest Hills Cemetery, are some of the works which speak of his untiring energy and genius. As early as 1811, he was appointed by the authorities of Boston to deliver the annual fourth-of-July address. It was full of fiery indignation at the insults and wrongs from Great Britain, and contained a glowing desire for such a monument to be built upon the Charlestown Hills as should commemorate the era which gave birth to a nation destined to be the most powerful on earth. From that day until the final consummation of that grandest monument in the world, he was untiring in its advocacy. A society was formed, with Webster as its president and Everett as its secretary, who labored for years with matchless eloquence for this great work. The act of incorporation named Dearborn as chairman of the committee to solicit subscriptions. The glow of his enthusiasm produced the first report, and his continuous efforts by tongue and pen kindled and kept alive the brains and hearts of those orators who stand confessedly at the head of the English-speaking tongue. Every gift of oratory and the muses, every appeal to patriotism, every effort of brave men and loving women was needed and exercised to produce that wonderful monument. Dearborn was chairman of the building committee for many years, and Judge Warren's history of the proceedings and debates, the dinners and suppers, the committee meetings and speeches of the eight men whom he calls the brightest galaxy that the country could produce—Webster, Story, Everett, Dearborn, J. C. Warren, Amos Lawrence, Gen. Sullivan, and George Blake—fills a portly volume of most interesting reading.* It was a task so vast and so difficult of accom-

---

* Warren's History of the Bunker-Hill Monument Association.

plishment, and came so near failure and defeat that I
think it safe to say that without the labors of either Webster, Everett, or Dearborn it never could have been accom
plished.*

A few weeks ago, in a speech at the Massachusetts
State Fair, Gov. Butler stated that the Hoosac Tunnel
was now a self-supporting and paying investment, and
that the direct increase of value to lands in that vicinity,
formerly almost valueless, was increased by actual assess-
ment several millions of dollars. This achievement was
due more largely to Gen. Dearborn than to any other man

* It is worthy of remembrance in this Society, which owes so much of its
existence to the Rev. Wm. Barry and his late accomplished wife, Elizabeth
Willard, vice-regent of the Mt. Vernon's Ladies Association, that the Bunker
Hill monument was built by her uncle, Solomon Willard. He was unanimously elected architect and superintendent at a full meeting of the building
committee, Oct. 3, 1825—Webster, Story, Everett, Dearborn, J. C. Warren,
Amos Lawrence, Gen. Wm. Sullivan, and George Blake (Warren's "Hist. of
Bunker-Hill Mon. Ass.," p. 199). Warren says: "Every one conceded to
him wonderful skill, ingenuity, and fidelity." The building of the monument
led to the construction of the first railroad in America, and Willard was one
of the incorporators in March, 1826. Warren says: "Willard refused all
compensation for his services, which lasted many years; and his services as
architect and superintendent at ordinary rates, and the amount he saved by
quarrying his own granite, and in other ways, equalled the whole actual cost
of the monument. The skill of Willard perfected the whole and made it
more majestic in its massive composition. He gave to it the strength and
maturity of his manhood, so that the very soul and fibre of his existence
were wrought into the mighty fabric from the foundation-stone to the airy
apex. In view of such sublime devotion, it may be hoped by us that as the
lover of art, when he visits Rome and views with admiration the dome of
St. Peters, recalls at once the exalted genius of Michael Angelo, so in future
ages will the visitor to Bunker Hill, as he gazes upon the imperishable obelisk
which crowns the metropolis, be reminded of the consummate skill and the
unmatched, priceless service of SOLOMON WILLARD."

Whoever reads Mrs. Barry's history of this Society (Blanchard's "Northwest," p. 457) will long remember the great services she and her husband
have rendered—not so conspicuous as those of her uncle, but no less enduring, perhaps—in the formation and endowment of the Chicago Historical
Society.

in New England. He was one of the earliest and most
indefatigable in his endeavors to induce the people of
Massachusetts to connect the Atlantic with the Hudson
River.

As early as 1838, he said, "It is the most remarkable
commercial avenue which was ever opened by man. It
has no parallel in the proudest days of antiquity, and in-
stead of the possibility of its ever being rivalled in any
country, it will itself be triplicated in extent, for the true
and ultimate terminus is to be on the shores of the Pacific
Ocean, and the splendid Alexandria of the Columbia
River will become the entrepot for the products of this
vast continent, of China and India, of Europe and Africa."

In a great railroad convention at Portland in 1850, he
said, "It is but twenty-five years since I proposed that a
railroad should be constructed from Boston to the Hudson, and that a tunnel be made through the Hoosac Mountain. For this I was termed an idiot. An idiot I may
be, but the road is made and the tunnel through the
Hoosac Mountain is in course of construction." He did
not live to see his desire accomplished.[*]

---

[*] While in Boston, seeking materials for this paper, I chanced to meet our
Col. Wentworth and Hon. A. W. H. Clapp of Portland, Me., who served
together in Congress. Mr. Clapp married the only daughter of Gen. H. A. S.
Dearborn. He told me that one of Dearborn's remarkable characteristics
was the accuracy and tenacity of his memory; and to illustrate this, narrated
the following anecdote: At the great railroad convention in Portland in 1850,
there were many delegates from the British Provinces, and among them was
an aged admiral of the British navy. Gen. Dearborn had never seen the
admiral; but, in the midst of an eloquent oration on the value of great highways of communication between different lands and nations, he wandered off
and described with great power and pathos a country and people somewhere,
long before, where the yellow fever or the cholera was raging to such an extent
that almost everybody who had the power to escape went away; but one
young officer, who, though fully at liberty to go, voluntarily staid by the
natives and fought death, disease, and horrors until the plague was staid; then
turning to the old admiral, whose tears were trickling down his face, Gen.

.

It has been my fortune during the last year to pass through the three greatest tunnels of the world the Hoosac, Mount Cenis, connecting France with Italy, and St. Gothard, connecting Switzerland and Germany with Italy. The last two wonderful works have been built in countries enjoying the accumulated skill and capital of two thousand years, and were aided by the governments of France, Italy, and Germany, and I thought with pride that the pioneer of these stupendous works was built by a State less than one century old, and owed its existence to the efforts of one ardent private citizen.

In 1838, he traveled extensively through our western country, and filled the Boston newspapers with glowing accounts of its natural resources, and stimulated the movement of Massachusetts' capital and citizens to this particular point.

His written and spoken contributions to the public, not one of which was written for personal reward or gain, would fill one hundred volumes. They covered the whole range of study and thought. Marshall P. Wilder says of him, "No enterprise was too bold for him to attempt, no sacrifice was too great for him to make, no labor too arduous for him to perform, in order to promote the intelligence, the refinement, welfare, and renown of his countrymen."*

Dearborn welcomed him, as the hero of his tale, to an American audience. Mr. Clapp said that later in the day both men were at his house at dinner, and when introduced, the admiral asked Gen Dearborn where he learned the particulars of that story. Gen. Dearborn answered, that he had read them in an obscure paper of New Brunswick, twenty-five years before, and the moment he heard the name of the admiral, all the details came back to his memory.

* I can not forbear making at least one quotation from Gen. Dearborn to show his flowing and eloquent style and as sounding the key-note of his character and principles. It is from an address in 1835, before the Massachusetts Society for promoting agriculture. He raises his subject at every paragraph

In 1829, a few gentlemen around Boston formed the present wealthy and successful Massachusetts Horticultural Society. Gen. Dearborn was its first president and continued such for many years. Its annual exhibitions, its fairs and banquets have been favored with some of the choicest hours and wittiest efforts of Webster, Story, and Everett. Dearborn and his successor, Marshall P. Wilder, had a way of infusing their own energy into all the men

from labor to triumph, from the soil to the flower, from the ground to the skies:

"There never has been anything great achieved where there were not difficulties to be encountered. It is thus that the noblest faculties of the mind have been wrought up to the exercise of their highest powers, and man to the display of his immeasurable resources. Every conception of an important truth is accompanied by the cheering belief of witnessing its verification; and the triumph over obstructions in its development is as exhilarating to the philosopher and artist as victory to the warrior. It matters not what is the exaggerated magnitude or apparent insignificance of the inquiry, it can not be prosecuted with any prospect of success, unless there is an ardent disposition, accompanied by that indomitable spirit of perseverance which puts at defiance all hazards and all odds. Whether the object of accomplishment or investigation be the construction of a Roman aqueduct or the stringing of a lute, the geology of the globe or the anatomy of a beetle, the discovery of a new world or a new plant, there must be brought into vigorous action the highest powers of intellect and the most zealous determination of purpose. There is nothing valuable to man or honorable to nations—not an addition has been made to the fund of intelligence—not a step taken in the progress of civilization, which has not been the result of intense thought and infinite research. It is one of the conditions of our existence—the fiat of Omnipotence—that to attain excellence in even the humblest vocation, there must be untiring industry, sanguine hopes, and great labor. What, indeed, were we but for that unquenchable thirst of knowledge which no acquisitions can abate—that restless demand for action, which is but increased by fruition, and that aspiring reach of imagination, which, finding no terrestrial bounds, ranges from the farthest constellation in the zodiac to the realms beyond the skies—to an existence as illimitable as eternity, and an elevation transcendant as the archangels. Were we not thus created and so endowed with an intuitive credence in the immortality of the soul, the human race must have remained in a state of the most abject ignorance and degraded barbarism. It is the inspiration of divinity itself which animates and urges us on in the interminable career of intellectual attainments and moral grandeur."

of genius in their vicinity. Dearborn possessed an insatiable love of the beautiful in nature and art. He studied every flower and fruit, every leaf and tree. His orations before that society and similar associations through New England awakened such an interest in horticulture that even before his death the rock-ribbed, rugged old State of Massachusetts became more beautifully embellished than the Northern Hesperides. Not only did the people near Boston clothe their whole earth with beauty, but as a practical business operation their exports of fruit increased a thousandfold.

The society which he erected is now one of the richest as well as one of the most useful in Boston. I had the pleasure of attending its annual exhibition held last September, and found an elegant stone temple filled with the richest profusion of flowers and fruits that any climate has yet produced. From the canvas-covered walls looked down a company of the most worthy men of Boston, and in the first place of honor was a portrait of its first president. That is just and well, but the real record of his genius and taste buds and flowers in all the fields and groves, the public parks and private walks of New England. As Dr. Putnam said, "There are thousands who may never speak his name, who unconsciously follow his teachings and copy his ideas in the flowers and trees that adorn their homes and delight their eyes. There is something of his influence in the bridal wreath that graces and gladdens the brow of beauty. There is something of it in the luscious fragrance of every basket of summer fruit that enriches the festive board. He, more than any one man, put in train those agencies which introduced to the knowledge and love of all classes of our people a greatly-extended variety both of the useful and ornamental products of the ground. He loved the beautiful and taught his countrymen to love it. He introduced new forms of

it and contributed to the permanent adorning of the fair
face of Nature."

It was from this exquisite taste of Dearborn and the
enthusiastic spirit and warm vitalizing eloquence, with
which he always carried captive the sympathetic and sus-
ceptible men with whom he came in contact, that our
whole Nation is indebted for an entire revolution in the
way of burying our dead. In 1829, there was no great
rural cemetery in this country nor in all Europe, excepting
Père La Chaise in Paris, but with Gen. Dearborn's accept-
ance of the presidency of the Massachusetts Horticultural
Society began a new era of sepulture.

Dr. Bigelow, Judge Story, Edward Everett, Abbot Lawrence, and other noble men of Boston had talked of a
rural cemetery, but when Dearborn took practical hold of
the matter, selected the ground, planned the improvements,
measured the walks and drives, then Mount Auburn was
born. Putnam says, "With an eye so keen to detect the
beautiful and a heart so warmly loving it, he knew how to
make the most of every nook and dell, the tangled bog,
the sandy level, the abrupt declivity, every tree and shrub
and rock—in a word, he, after God, created Mount Auburn.
His zeal and vigor, taste and labor, were the most prominent and efficacious elements in the inception and accomplishment of the work. And there lies Mount Auburn
with its sacred beauty, its holy fitness for its object, with
its quiet enclosure, its solemn and tender associations, its
thousands of gleaming monuments, itself in its entireness
a magnificent and beautiful monument to him, to his industry and taste—his affectionate reverence for the claims
of the dead and the sorrows of the living."

But not here alone; the hills of Roxbury, where Washington's cannon once commanded the British army to eva-
cuate Boston, offered still greater natural beauties to Dearborn's artistic eye, and he spent not only months but years

in developing and beautifying there the Forest-Hills Cemetery. He planned it all and superintended it all, not for
pay, but for pure love of work and its results. From
these exquisite models of gardens for the dead sprang
similar rural cemeteries all over our country, until every
city and village vied with each other in the sacred work.
I remember well how early my own love for such places
was awakened. In 1850, I attended the dedication of the
cemetery at Utica, N.Y., when Mr. William Tracy was the
orator to a throng of the most gifted men of Oneida.
There were present the Spensers, Denios, Kirklands, Sey-
mours, Johnstons, Bacons, Roscoe Conkling and the old
chief of the Oneidas, nearly one hundred years of age. I
have visited Mount Auburn, Greenwood, Laurel Hill, Fort
Hill, Mount Hope, and nearly every cemetery between
Boston and Buffalo, all of which places, being the highest
in their vicinity, were once the scenes of Revolutionary
conflict, and are now dotted with monuments of our dead
warriors of many wars. I remember, too, my visit to Père
La Chaise,* to visit the unmarked grave of Marshal Ney,
where we chanced to meet old Victor Hugo bearing
his last son to his tomb,—old Victor Hugo, whose
description of Waterloo will be read and admired so long
as a militant world exists; but none of these visits im-

* On the 28th of December, 1873, I visited this famous cemetery in company with Mr. S. H. K., Jr., and his mother, whose thorough culture and
historical information made every hour agreeable and instructive.
We had been to the Hotel Dieu, the oldest hospital in Europe, and to Hospital Lariboissière, the great modern hospital for the poor. All the avenues
leading to Père La Chaise were unusually crowded. After we had visited the
graves of Marshals Ney, Davoust, and Massena, the poet Beranger, and the
garlanded sarcophagus of Abelard and Eloise, we turned to leave the cemetery
and were met by an immense funeral procession, headed by Victor Hugo,
then about seventy-two years of age, coming to bury the last of his children,
François Victor Hugo, the translator of Shakespeare and a man of the highest
promise. With him walked Gambetta, Alexandre Dumas, Jules Simon, and
a host of the leading men of France. Louis Blanc pronounced a touching

pressed me as did that to the graves of these Dearborns at
Forest-Hills Cemetery.   They lie on the highest ground of
that eminence, with beautiful monumental marbles erected
by a grateful public to their memory.   It was a soft and
lovely September-Sunday sunset, and as I thought of the
brave and generous and gifted laborers, who, after so much
work in their country's service, slept their last sleep within
sound of the city's roar and the ocean's swell, it seemed
as though the requiem which vibrated from the trees over
their graves was carried from hill to hill, from the Atlantic
Ocean to our own resounding shore at Graceland.*

oration by the side of the old man, and expressed the sympathies which
throbbed through the hearts of all Paris.

Surrounded by the tombs of the most famous of the sons of France of this
century, and by the living celebrities of the new Republic, we looked upon
the bowed head of Victor Hugo, and forgot in him the statesman, the poet,
the orator, in utter pity for the *man*—for the father—who had given to Père
La Chaise the last of his children.   The great philanthropist had claimed for
forty years that "all humanity was his family."   He now stood without father,
mother, sister, brother, wife, or child, and while he wept, "all humanity"
shared his sorrow and took him into its inmost heart.

* If there was a name more thoroughly embalmed in the hearts of the
patriots than all others, it was that of Gen. Joseph Warren, who fell at the
battle of Bunker Hill.   Orators, poets, and painters have vied with each
other to honor his memory.   At Forest-Hills Cemetery, on the summits of
two adjoining hills called Mount Warren and Mount Dearborn, repose the
bones of those two physicians who fought together in 1775.   A deep dell of
exquisite loveliness runs between the two heights.   In the first annual report
of the Forest-Hills commissioners, Gen. H. A. S. Dearborn suggested the pro-
priety of erecting a bronze statue of Warren on this hill, named in his honor,
and near which he was born and lived.   In this connection it is interesting to
note that within a hundred yards of this Hall resides a venerable lady, Mrs.
Mary P. Tucker (mother of Mr. Joseph F. Tucker, a member of this Society),
whose father, Professor Hezekiah Packard, was in that famous battle of 1775,
was present when the remains of Warren were removed from the battle-field,
and was present in 1825 when Lafayette laid the corner-stone of the monument and Webster delivered his immortal oration.

One of the officers and active members of the Bunker-Hill-Monument Association was Franklin Dexter, whose widow is a granddaughter of Col. Prescott,
the commander at the battle.   This venerable lady was present on the 17th
June, 1881, when the beautiful bronze statue of Col. Prescott was unveiled
and Robert C. Winthrop delivered his masterly oration.

There are few names in our history which better represent in two generations the record and terrible experiences of war and the beaming and beautiful works of peace than the Dearborns—few men in two succeeding generations of father and son whose history so fully represents the military, political, social, and business operations and vicissitudes of America.

The first sprang into undying fame when he hurried over the public highway from New Hampshire to Cambridge after the echo of the guns from Lexington, and took his baptism of fire and blood on Bunker Hill. The younger gathered his laurels when "grim-visaged war had smoothed his wrinkled front"; when his Country was at peace with the world, and through the pleasant ways of commerce, of art, of letters, of flowers and fruit and poetry, he walked through a long life of companionship with the most gifted scholars and orators our Country has produced. The turbulent energy of all classes of men during our contest for independence had not become enervated by luxury, and though the younger Dearborn found fortune smiling and a liberal income flowing into his treasury, he carried into and through his own generation the restless energy which he inherited from the warrior of the Revolution, and work of every kind was to him the very breath of life. He studied all science, all art, all commerce, all literature; he brought home to the minds of men the vast possibilities which lay before our Country in the West; and to the hearts of lovers of the beautiful, the creations of fancy and the delights of a beautiful home and an unrepulsive grave. He, more than any other man in New England, made the rock-ribbed homesteads of his neighborhood to blossom with flowers and fruits, and its graves to perpetuate in external beauty the loftiest ideals of those who came to visit their treasures.

The career of the father coming upon the stage from

the sulphur call of Lexington, rolling back the flower of British veterans with the most deadly destruction ever to that period experienced, and never before or since approached, except at New Orleans; marching, swimming, starving from Cambridge to Quebec, leading his men against the Gibraltar of Canada, made immortal by Wolfe and Montgomery; leading his New-Hampshire boys with the mad Arnold and the heroic Scammel to the great victory of Saratoga; then beneath the eye of his peerless friend and hero on the bloody field of Monmouth; and on and on to the glorious culmination at Yorktown: — that career seems like the great roll of a thunder-storm, before which one stands mute, feeling that the circumstances and consequences are all phenomenal, and that none but the great God of battles can know what shall come next. But the career of the son seems like a beautiful river flowing through a country at first wild and unnavigable, like his own Kennebec or Merrimac, carrying beauty and life through all its hills and mountains, its fields and gardens, washing the rural homes of men who have learned to love Nature for its own sake, proud of their ancestry and looking fondly at faces and forms made real to them by the brush of Copley, Trumbull, and Stuart; homes where "plenty leaps to laughing life" under the touch of industry; and where such brains and hearts as Longfellow, Lowell, Hawthorne, Holmes, Whittier, Dana, Emerson, and Winthrop fill the every-day of their sphere with love and sentiment tuned to harmony.

Some of you have known and witnessed similar careers to the elder Dearborn, but twenty years of peace and prosperity have made us feel that organized and hellish passion will never again drench our land in blood or fire our forts and capitals with flame; and so I repeat, the career of the father is phenomenal, and we hope need not again be developed in America.

But the career of the younger Dearborn is an example which all can imitate. His energy, like the steam-locomotive which he prophesied fifty years ago would yet travel from ocean to ocean, will never seem common; his exquisite taste will be the gift only of the few; but no well-born American need despair of approximating a career whose chief trait was good-will to all, and a desire to make the world richer by commerce, easier by science, and more lovely by flowers surrounding every home and embellishing every grave.

At the close of Mr. Goodwin's lecture, Hon. John Went-worth moved that the thanks of the Society be tendered to Mr. Goodwin for his able and interesting address, and that a copy of the same be requested to be placed in the archives of the Society. And he wished the audience would excuse him for saying that he hoped that the research that Mr. Goodwin had manifested, and that the very interesting manner in which he has handled his subject would be a model for other lectures.

"Some of our lectures abound in facts; but these facts are not handled in a manner to make them interesting, whilst other lectures abound in eloquent expressions without the facts to make them instructive. This lecture will bear repeating; and if Mr. Goodwin was only a professional, it would be a good one to travel over the country with. I am surprised that we have never heard from Mr. Goodwin before, and I hope we shall often hear from him hereafter. I see many around me who are in the habit of passing their summers in the vicinity of Hampton, N. H., at the ocean beach, where the birthplace of Gen. Dearborn is pointed out. Since this lecture, that place will possess additional interest.

"Having expressed my views elaborately as to the public services of Gen. Dearborn, at the unveiling of the Memorial Tablet to mark the site of old Fort Dearborn, 21 May, 1881, I will say no more of him than that history records no other man who was at the battle of Bunker Hill, the surrenders of Burgoyne and Cornwallis, and then took an active part in the war of 1812. He was among the very first men to respond to the call of his country, and among the very last to leave the field of battle. I doubt if there has been a man of such humble pretentions with so valuable and long-continued public services. Although born and raised in the same State with Gen. Dearborn, and familiar from childhood with the region

from which he so promptly started after hearing of the
battle of Lexington, I have no remembrance of ever seeing him, as he died June 6, 1829; but his son, Gen. Henry
Alexander Scammell Dearborn, who studied law with my
professor whilst I was at the Harvard Law University,
Justice Joseph Storey, I was well acquainted with. When
that son-in-law of his, who also now lives at Portland,
Maine, so full of honors and of the respect of all who
know him, Hon. Asa W. H. Clapp, was in Congress, he
was often at Washington and I often met him in Boston,
and he was at least once in Chicago. He was a man of
resolution, of great industry, varied tastes and acquire-
ments—one of those rare men who could gain a reputation
in handling any matter to which his attention might be
called. He was a Massachusetts State senator, a congress-
man, a collector of customs, a soldier of the war of 1812,
mayor of Roxbury, and an author of great repute. His
'Life of Christ' was in advance of anything of the kind
of his day; but its want of denominational bias kept it
from that publicity to which his research and talents
entitled it.

"Mr. President:—I consider that it is one of the main
objects of historical societies to connect the past with the
present, and I am always pleased when I can mention
some living descendant of the honored men concerning
whom this society is addressed. There is but one descendant bearing the name of these two honored Gens. Dearborn, Henry George Raleigh Dearborn of Roxbury, Mass.,
a resident of Chicago in 1838, and afterward of Winnebago
County, in this State. There was no one of our early set-
tlers more respected and now more favorably remembered
than Henry Thurston of Harlaem, Winnebago County, an
emigrant from Lancaster, Mass. Mr. Dearborn married
his daughter, Sarah M., July 6, 1840, a sister of Mrs.
Elizabeth Thurston, who died in this city, April 20, 1879,

the wife of our respected fellow-citizen, Stephen W. Clary, and also sister of John H. Thurston, a prominent merchant of Rockford, Ill.

"One of the highest compliments paid to Gen. Dearborn is the fact that whilst the names of so many of our streets have been changed to gratify the whims of our aldermen, no attempt has been made to change that of Dearborn Street. Not only is this the case, but the name of Dearborn continues to be prefixed to institutions, enterprises, and objects which it is the desire of projectors to honor."

Hon. J. Young Scammon said:

"I rise to second the motion of Colonel Wentworth. I was not, like him and General Henry Dearborn, a native of the Granite State; but my father was. My father, Eliakim Scammon, like General Dearborn, emigrated to the Kennebec country in Maine at an early day, when it was the District of Maine, and both settled in the same town, where the early days of my childhood and youth were spent. My father lived in the eastern part of the town, known as East Pittston, about seven miles from the Kennebec River. The Dearborn farm was in the west portion of the town, occupying a high and commanding situation not far from the river. The village of that part of Pittston, called Gardiner, after the separation and incorporation of the latter, became a centre of trade; and at this point was the ferry, which was on the great road from the Kennebec to the Damariscotta and Sheepscot Rivers, and the salt water in the direction toward the old town of Wiscasset, the county-seat of Lincoln Co. General Dearborn formerly lived in a large two-story house in Gardiner, opposite and almost directly in front of the ferry landing. His farm on the other side of the river was kept in fine order and well stocked. It was a pattern farm. I frequently passed it. I recollect how my childish curi-

osity was gratified by the novel sight in that country of a
donkey, which the General sent home from Portugal when
he was minister to that kingdom.

"My grandfather, David Young, like General Dearborn,
was in the Revolutionary War, and among our forces
which went to Canada to attack Quebec. He was in
Arnold's expedition which went up the Kennebec River.
Our family, like General Dearborn's, was in politics Jeffer-
sonian - Republicans, as distinguished from the Federal
Republicans, and always took an interest in political
affairs. The Dearborns, Youngs, and Scammons were all
devoted Republicans. My grandfather represented his
town in the general court of Massachusetts, before the
separation, as General Dearborn did in Congress the representative district in which it was situated.

"I do not recollect ever seeing Gen. Henry Dearborn,
though I may have done so. His son, Gen. Henry A. S.
Dearborn, I knew, and have seen him in Chicago. He, at
one time, about 1838 probably, came to Jacksonville, in
this State, with a view of making his home here; but he
found the country entirely too new for his habits of life,
and left at once for his old home in Massachusetts. When
I subsequently met him, it was in Hubbard & Co.'s
warehouse on North-Water Street. He had then, I
think, been out to visit his son on Rock River. He was
a very remarkable as well as distinguished man. His
spare time and thoughts were devoted to matters of
public and general interest, and he was one of the very
few men who saw, before the days of railroads with us,
the great advantage of quick and rapid communication
between the lake region and the seaboard. I never pass
Booth's great piscatory establishment at the corner of
Lake and State Streets, which is usually overflowing with
the productions of the waters from Oregon and the Columbia River to the coast of Maine and the Penobscot, without

4

being reminded that the 'young general', as he was called, said to me, on the occasion referred to in Hubbard & Co.'s warehouse, that railroad communication with the East would not only furnish us a market for our cereals and other productions, but in return would also bring us fresh food for our table from the briny deep. I was at that time greatly interested in promoting railroad communication with the East, preparatory to extending our contemplated roads to the Northwest. The impression he made upon me at that short interview has remained to this day.

"I knew his three sisters. One was married to Hon. Joshua Wingate, formerly of Bath, Maine, a member of Congress at one time, I think, from the Lincoln district. He subsequently removed to Portland, having been appointed collector of U. S. customs for that district. The other two sisters were married in Pittston, one to Dr. James Parker, who was a senator in the general court of Massachusetts, and a Republican member of Congress before the separation. The other sister, I think a half-sister, was married to Mr. Rufus Gay, for many years a successful merchant in Pittston and Gardiner. For the last three years before I left Maine, in 1835, they resided in Gardiner. I was in the habit on Sundays of attending a small religious meeting in Gardiner, to which the Parkers and Gays both belonged. Sympathy of belief created intimate association, and there were probably few months during this period that I was not hospitably entertained at one or other of these houses on Sunday. These memories are among the red-letter days of my life.

"The name Dearborn has a double charm for me. It was associated with all the days of my youth and early manhood, and though neither the Dearborn Block nor the Dearborn Observatory at the Chicago University was named for General Dearborn, they were for a distant relative around whose name cluster all the blissful associations of my early Chicago life.

"I thank the orator of the evening not only for the honor he has done to my ancestral home and its early inhabitants, for the faithful and careful labor which has produced so true and faithful historical portraits of the two distinguished General Dearborns, but for the rare skill and grace in which he has set those presentations. Never have we listened in this hall to a more interesting paper. In his paper he combined the orator, the historian, and the essayist. It is an honor to us and to our institution."

Hon. E. B. Washburne said, while offering this vote of thanks to Mr. Goodwin, which was so appropriate and well deserved, he thought there should be added a resolution tendering the warmest thanks and gratitude of the Society to the gentlemen whose liberality had secured the admirable portrait of General Dearborn, which was hereafter to adorn our walls. Connected as the name of General Dearborn was so intimately with Chicago, the gift of his portrait would always be gratefully remembered. He begged, therefore, to move that the cordial thanks of the Society be tendered to the donors, whose names were on the tablet.

Hon. Isaac N. Arnold, president of the Society, said:

"Before submitting the resolutions, I can not forbear expressing the great pleasure with which I have listened to the paper which has been read. The subject has not only great local but national interest, and the treatment has been admirable. Many very interesting papers have been read before our Society, but I am sure all will agree with me that it is rare for this, or, indeed, any Historical Society in the country to listen to one of such merit. It is a prose-poem with the accuracy of history. Mr. Goodwin has united the picturesque description and glowing sentiment of poetry and eloquence,"

Mr. Arnold then put the question on the resolutions and they were unanimously adopted and the meeting adjourned.

Letter from Hon. Robert C. Winthrop, president of the Massachusetts Historical Society:

"BOSTON, 26th Dec., 1883.

"DEAR MR. GOODWIN:

"I received and have read with interest your account of the Dearborns in a Chicago newspaper of the 19 inst. You will doubtless publish the whole of your paper in pamphlet, and I shall be glad to have a copy. My relations with both the Generals were close. The father's last wife was my mother's aunt, Mrs. Sarah Bowdoin—the widow of James Bowdoin, son of Governor Bowdoin. She was herself a Bowdoin, the only cousin of her first husband and niece of your wife's ancestress, Elizabeth Bowdoin Pitts.

"My father's family always dined with the Dearborns on Thanksgiving Day and the Dearborns always dined at my father's on Christmas Day. They were our nearest of kin at that time in Boston, and rarely a week passed without their being at our house.

"The younger General Dearborn was adjutant-general of Massachusetts while I was aide-de-camp of more than one of our governors—Davis, Armstrong, and Everett—and we were much together on parade days and at reviews. They were noble men—father and son—for whom I had a warm regard.   Yours truly,

"ROB'T C. WINTHROP."

HAWTHORN COTTAGE, BOSTON HIGHLANDS,
January 7th, 1884.

MY DEAR SIR:—Allow me to thank you for the great
pleasure the perusal of the sketches of my beloved and
honored father and grandfather have given myself and
family. Your treatment of the subject, I think, has
evinced great good taste and judgment in the selection
of the most important and interesting periods in their
history.

I feel under great obligations to you and the gentlemen
associated with you.

The portrait by Gilbert Stuart was painted in 1812. Of
the six attempts that have been made to copy it, this is
the most satisfactory. It gives me great pleasure to know
that a portrait of my grandfather is in the Chicago Historical Society.

My family unite with me in kind regards.

Very respectfully,

H. G. R. DEARBORN.

DANIEL GOODWIN, Jr.

INDEX.

Reid, Gen. George, 20.

S.

Saratoga, battle of, 14, 15.
Scammon, J. Young, remarks, 48.
Scammon, Eliakim, 48.
Scammell, Col. Alexander, 14, 18, 19.
Scott, Gen. Winfield, 30, 32.
Skinner, Mark, 3.
Stark, Col. John, 11.
Story, Justice Joseph, 22, 25, 34, 40, 45, 47.
Strong, Gov. Caleb, 27, 28.
Strong, Elder John's descendants, 28 n.
Strong, Gen. William Emerson, 28 n.
Stuart, Gilbert, 2, 44, 53.
Sullivan, Gen. and Gov. James, 18, 19, 22, 32.
Sullivan, Gen. William, 34.

T.

Talleyrand, 22.
Thurston, Henry, 45, 47.
Thurston, John H., 48.
Ticonderoga, 14.
Tracy, Wm., orator at Utica, 41.
Tucker, Joseph F., 42.

Tucker, Mrs. Mary P., 42.
Tuthill, Richard Stanley, 28 n.

W.

Warner, Col. and Mrs. Jonathan, 21.
Warren, Judge George W., 34.
Warren, Dr. J. C., 34.
Warren, Gen. Joseph, 42.
Washington, President, 3, 7, 17, 18, 22.
Waterman, James Shields, 3.
Washburne, E. B., remarks, 51.
Webster, Daniel, 17, 23, 34.
Wentworth, Col. John, 3, 23, 25, 36; remarks, 46; genealogy quoted, 21.
Whistler, Capt. John, 3, 16, 24.
Willard, Solomon, 35.
Williams, Gen. A. S., 22.
Wilson, Gen. James Grant, 24, 25.
Wingate, Gen. Joshua W., 50.
Wingate, Mrs., 32, 50.
Wilder, Marshall P., 37, 38.
Winthrop, Robert C., 32, 42, 44, 52.

Y.

Yorktown, 19, 32.
Young, David, 49.